Developing a Champion
SPIRIT
In just 10 minutes

For Men Only

Mikel Brown

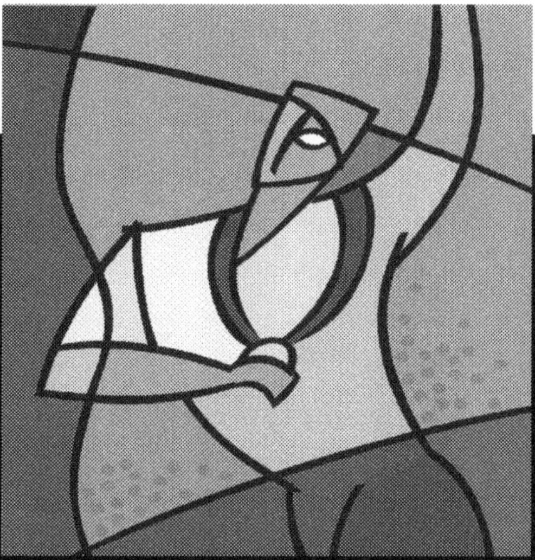

Developing a Champion
SPIRIT
In just 10 minutes

For Men Only

Mikel Brown

EL PASO, TEXAS

Developing the Champion Spirit in just 10 minutes

For Men Only

CJC PUBLISHING COMPANY

1208 Sumac Drive
El Paso, TX 79925

Copyright © 2005 by Mikel Brown
Printed in the United States of America
Library of Congress Control Number: 2005926812
ISBN: 1-930388-11-X

Editorial assistance for CJC Publishing Co. by Gary Sparkman

All scriptures are taken from the King James Version and the New International Version

Cover design by C. Hughes Advertising Agency

Published by CJC Publishing Company

All rights reserved. No portion of this book may be used without the written permission of the publisher, with the exception of brief excerpts in magazine articles, reviews, etc. For further information or permission, address CJC Publishing Co. 1208 Sumac Drive, El Paso, Texas 79925

FIRST EDITION - 2ND REVISION

Table of Contents

DEDICATION V

SPECIAL THANKS VI

PREFACE VII

CHAPTER 1
Developing the Champion in You...2

CHAPTER 2
Changing Men in Changing Times 21

CHAPTER 3
The Portrait of a Leader...30

CHAPTER 4
Exercising Your Power to Dominate...................................38

CHAPTER 5
Principles for Commanding Mountains And
Overcoming Obstacles...52

MEDALLIONS OF HONOR 61

NOTES..63

ABOUT THE AUTHOR 65

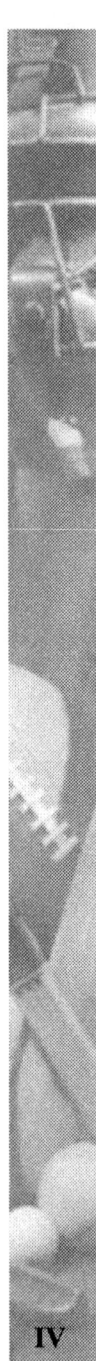

IV

Dedication

To my lifelong friend and wife for her unselfish devotion to me and my calling. To my children Joshua, Mikayla, Mikelle, Marquita, and Mikel Jr. who are part of the generation to which I've dedicated my efforts: to the many people whose lives will be touched and forever changed after reading this book.

Special Thanks

My heartfelt thanks and deepest appreciation to the following spiritual sons and daughters, and friends whose financial seeds have enabled the consummation of this project. I Love You!

Savaslas & Tracey Lofton (Music in my ear)
Derrick & Varonica Jones
Alan & Alma Spence
Reggie & Nancy Mainor
Scott & Laura Whittle
Roy & Tish Times
Gregory & Monica Austin
Bryan & Tracie Reed
Jameelah Joshua
Willie & Katherine Jenkins
Bill & Becky Smith

Preface

Dr. Mikel Brown usually starts his lectures by saying, "Hi, I'm Mikel Brown and it's good to be a winner!" Winning in life doesn't always equate to winning a contest. A contest of sports or games are not as important as life itself. One thing is for certain, no one really enjoys losing. When life seems to be going in a downward spiral, you need to quickly figure out how to get your life back on the up swing. It might seem incredible that you can turn your situation around, but everywhere people are raving about Dr. Mikel Brown's amazing tips on how to develop a winning edge. ***"Developing a Champion Spirit: In just Ten Minutes"*** will give you the tools and tactical approach on how YOU can be a Winner in Life.

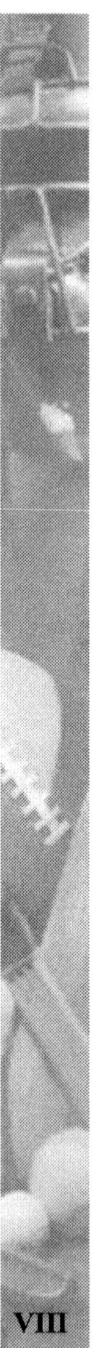

VIII

Chapter 1

Developing the Champion in You

Chapter 1

Developing the Champion in You

It doesn't take long to develop a Champion's Spirit; it simply takes patience to allow the process to unfold. Integrity, Character, Strength, and Leadership are four qualities that define a Champion. Personally, I'd rather be in control rather than under the control of someone else. Accepting the condition of being under control may suggest a mindset toward passivity. However, the desire to control your own destiny would tend to imply an inward proclivity toward an assertive disposition. People will basically subscribe to one of two worldviews regarding their lot in life. The first view places them in complete control of their environment, while individuals in the other category see themselves as the ruled, with little control over their existence. There is a vast difference between the two viewpoints.

Your struggles in life must be viewed as assignments, designed to expose your weaknesses so that you can expel them from your life. The struggles surface to prepare you for subsequent tests along the path of your destiny. You should never take life's tests without first studying your assignment. We have all, at some point in our lives, held secret fears of not being able to live up to the images we have projected to others. People are always looking for admiration and respect from others. The problem is that while we are learning how to be individuals of courage and integrity, we must do so in a world full of compromise. Champions are not those who never fail; they are those who never quit. Men and women who have never failed are usually those who have never set their minds to do anything. The difference between people who succeed and those who fail lies in their ability to handle the pressures that mount against them.

Character is defined by more than just talent and ability. Everyone has talent, but not everyone has character. Each of us must summons the courage to rely upon the integrity that resides deep within the heart of all of us. Everyone has his or her own core character values, and no one can duplicate anyone else's. The appeal of strong character serves to attract those searching for a fixed standard of excellence.

Within each of us lie amazing qualities that are not easily discerned. However, you must be tenacious enough to dig beneath the debris of failure, hurt and discouragement to find your hidden treasure. You must not tire in your quest to discover it. Perseverance will greatly assist you in your pursuits.

The bully whom you must face in life today as an adult is not necessarily the big, bad neighbor down the street. At this stage, the bully comes in the form of procrastination, bad habits, intimidation, negativity, unfortunate past childhood experiences, and cowardice; they are all designed to test your resolve to win in life.

Your life will not improve simply because you hope for it. It will only get better after you take the necessary steps to bring about the type of change you desire. If you do not exercise and eat right, your body will not function optimally. The same principle holds true in life. In order to make life work for you, you must apply certain principles and be willing to learn. It doesn't take long to develop a Champion's Spirit; it simply takes patience to allow the process to unfold.

C is for Courage

Valor doesn't mean that you are invincible, it just indicates that you have the audacity to stand in the face of the opposition and declare your position.

We live in a world where attempts at success are rewarded the same as the actual achievement. In actuality, no frail attempts at victory have ever produced winning results. Each year thousands of men and women join our armed forces and swear an oath to defend our constitution. However, when the time comes to actually fulfill their oaths, some then choose to conveniently declare conscientious objector status. The amazing part is that they never object to receiving any of the benefits that go along with wearing the uniform. Yet these same military personnel would stand in line for hours to receive a Purple Heart - - - for a yellow back.

A Champion must have the fortitude to follow through with commitment. Courage is always tested, or how else can we recognize its authenticity. The mistaken belief is that brave individuals face their opposition because they lack fear. The contrary is true. By overcoming their fears to face their opponents, individuals are then recognized as brave. To become brave, you must, at some point in your life, realize that it is better to fight on your feet than to serve on your knees.

Power words for Courage: bravery, courageousness, daring, dauntlessness, doughtiness, fearlessness, gallantry, guts, hardihood, heart, heroism, intrepidity, intrepidness, nerve, stoutness, valor, backbone, fortitude, grit, gumption, spunk, determination, perseverance, resolution, endurance, stamina, tenacity, audacity, boldness, brazenness, cheek, gall, temerity.

H is for Honor

Honor is the high estimation of a person who has gained the respect, consideration and veneration for doing what comes normal for them.

That which rightfully attracts esteem, respect, or consideration is not what you do, but how you do it! Athletes learn early on how to employ dirty tactics to gain the advantage against their opponents. However, if they are guided by an inward standard of self-respect, they will learn to accept winning or losing according to set rules.

Self-respect is better than people's respect. If you honor yourself, you will command respect from others without ever saying a word. When I look at people, I focus not only on physical appearances, but also on how people comport themselves. The person with nothing to prove is not overly concerned with what others think of him or her. This person refuses to live according to expectations of others.

A title is not honor, it's a label. Honor is an ornament of excellence and distinction. People of honor will put in the hours necessary to make their lives, marriages, businesses, churches, and relationships work. They know that it is not what you do that earns people's respect; it's simply how you do it.

Power words for Honor: dignity, courage, fidelity, especially, excellence of character, high moral worth, virtue, nobleness, integrity, uprightness, trustworthiness, in women, purity, chastity.

A is for Authority

When you recognize your power or authority, you must also identify the scope of it as well.

You have an ordained right to govern your life and live it as you choose. It is unfortunate, however, when people look to others to captain their lives. You are in your own custody, and you have the power to make all

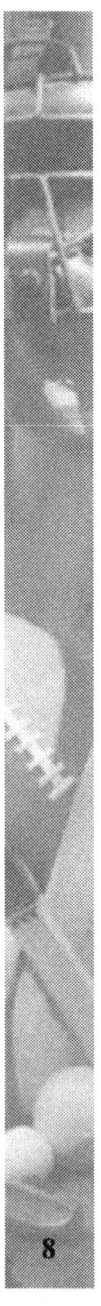

decisions concerning your life.

Power is weakness in the hands of the one who does not recognize its potential. Each person is in position to make his or her world into what is desired. However, millions of people would consciously leave their lives in the hands of fate. "Whatever will be, will be!" is their motto. This should not be the mantra that governs your life. It should actually be "Whatever you want to be, will be!"

You have the right to command how you want your life to turn out. Champions understand, by virtue of their status as humans, that they own the right to determine their course in life. As long as your brain is working, and your body is functional, people must learn to pilot their own lives. You can make your world as small or as large as you would like for it to be. That decision-making authority rests within each of us.

Power is simply authority, and authority must have its jurisdiction. Parents have jurisdiction over the life of their children. From this, we cannot conclude that the two people who are biologically responsible for producing a child are also the parents of that child. Parenthood implies so much more. In essence, the parents are the ones who feed, nurture, clothe, and educate their children. Dead beat mothers and dads are not parents in the true sense of the word. A true champion understands the areas where improvement is needed, even if improvement means facing embarrassing and humiliating circumstances for the purpose of teaching their children the importance of taking responsibility for one's actions.

People are not relegated to failure for the rest of their lives because they may have made some bad decisions. Get up from your despondent position and use your authority to turn your life around. Speak to your situation and command it to dissolve and dry up from the roots.

Power words for Authority: Legal, power, command, ability, strength, clout, influence, right, compel, force, and energy.

M is for Maturity

When a person can live with his or her past without being bogged down by it, he or she remains adaptable and capable to continue the process of change for a better life.

If an individual is going to grow toward the type of maturity that will foster a healthy self-esteem, it can only be built on a solid and unyielding foundation. Two major characteristics of maturity are the presence of wisdom and knowledge. They will help the person to be at home with realities, and not slide into a fantasy world of the make believe.

A child sees a puddle of water and jumps right into the middle of it, spattering water every where. A mature minded person sees the puddle of water and walks around it. This may sound simple to you now, but I assure you that when you were a young kid, the puddle of water was very tempting.

How a person handles responsibility reveals the level of their maturity. Taking responsibility for one's actions is a strong predictor of whether one will succeed in business and in life. Mature individuals can be ribald or genteel, sweet or acid, cheerful or gloomy, but the important point is that they be alive, with vigorous interests that make them interesting to be with. They should have a sense of humor because it helps to dilute the frustrations that one may encounter.

The mature person knows that he has to go on making decisions that are of little importance and of great importance; and that each option will cost him something. He knows that his integrity is continually susceptible to practical demands, seductive temptations, concessions, compromises and conflicting values, but that it can only be preserved at the cost of some

spiritual and mental energy being exerted.
Power words for Maturity: Realistic, decisive, responsible, developed, accountable, dependable, sensible, level-hearted, conscientious, and constant.

P is for Principles

The level of your present quality of life is all based on the principles you choose to be governed by.

The choices people make are influenced by their individual belief system. Principles are nothing more than a governing system of beliefs established by an individual that determines life's choices. Every principle is not necessarily a good principle. Principles govern all of our actions—even if the action is good, bad, or indifferent. When people say that they have morals, they are actually saying that they live by principles.

The principle of success is revealed in the mechanics of it. If a person desires to be successful, they must learn how success works. Success does not happen inadvertently as though one succeeds in spite of being ignorant. It is a deliberate attempt to follow through on the rules of engagement concerning success. If success is a game, then there must be rules or laws that dictate how it is played...rules that will guarantee your success every time.

> "I hated every minute of training, but I said, 'Don't quit. Suffer now and live the rest of your life as a champion." —Muhammad Ali

Aristotle said "Excellence is not an act, but a habit." I am a firm believer that success is not an accident. Unlike millions of Americans, who play the lottery in hopes that they will one day buy the winning ticket, I believe that I am the winning ticket. My future will rise or fall on my willingness to submit to the regimen of preparation that will lead me to success. Every winner in life has one common trait; they have learned to master the fundamentals or principles.

A boxer who is vigorous in his training realizes that victory comes in the training, and not in the actual fight. Your willingness to prepare and to be coached or mentored is evidence of your passion and desire to succeed. You cannot escape this fundamental principle of success. If a person's marriage fails or if a business does not succeed, you better believe that those failures can be traced back to either refusing to listen to sound counsel or refusing to adhere to the principles that are necessary to finish what was started.

A champion has all the traits of a winner. They

have qualified and employed the services of a key person (life coach) who has a proven track record of providing sound, results-producing counsel regarding matters of interest. The qualified mentor or life coach must have an established belief system based on truth and not fantasy. It should be evident that they have engaged their mental faculty for both the development of their body and sound habits. They are people of principles and not preference. Preferences are negotiable, but principles are non-negotiable.

Power words for Principles: truth, basics, essentials, fundamentals, rudiments, foundation, groundwork, nitty-gritty, belief, canon, doctrine, dogma, faith, philosophy, axiom, law, precept, tenet, rule, and standard.

I is for Integrity

The integrity of a person is not just in their ability to speak the truth, but also in their power to live it.

Integrity seems to be a dying art in society. The quality or the state of being complete is integrity in force. Soundness and sobriety are qualities that are tantamount to integrity and should be viewed as an essential component to a person's success.

Developing A Champion Spirit – in just 10 minutes

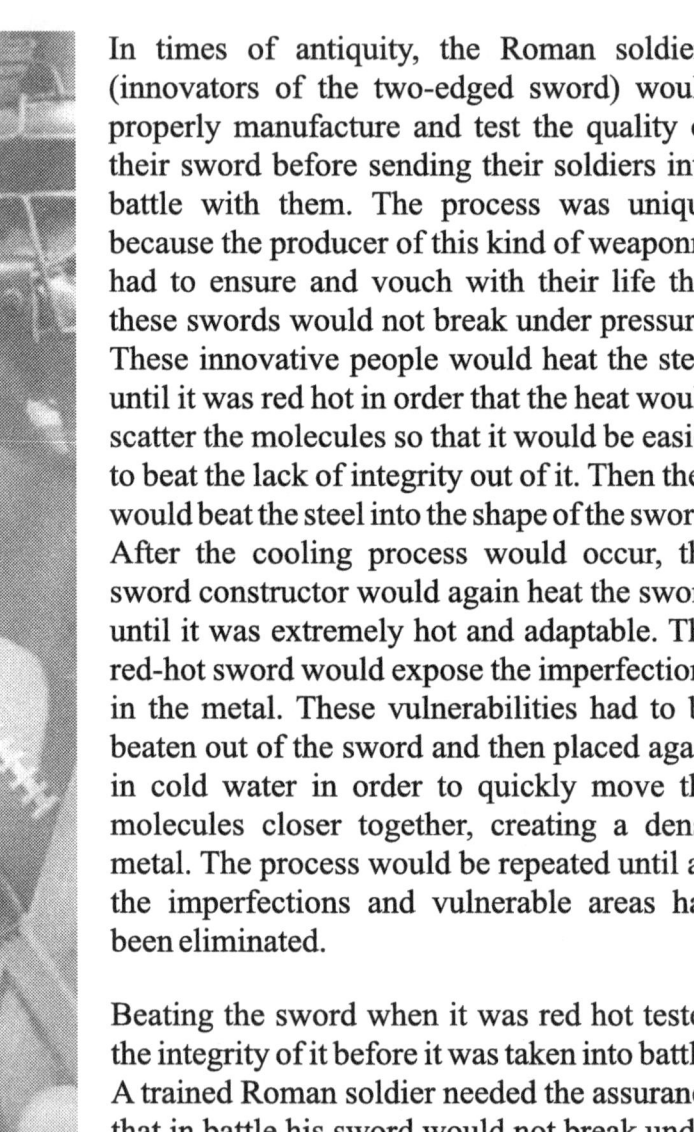

In times of antiquity, the Roman soldiers (innovators of the two-edged sword) would properly manufacture and test the quality of their sword before sending their soldiers into battle with them. The process was unique because the producer of this kind of weaponry had to ensure and vouch with their life that these swords would not break under pressure. These innovative people would heat the steel until it was red hot in order that the heat would scatter the molecules so that it would be easier to beat the lack of integrity out of it. Then they would beat the steel into the shape of the sword. After the cooling process would occur, the sword constructor would again heat the sword until it was extremely hot and adaptable. The red-hot sword would expose the imperfections in the metal. These vulnerabilities had to be beaten out of the sword and then placed again in cold water in order to quickly move the molecules closer together, creating a dense metal. The process would be repeated until all the imperfections and vulnerable areas had been eliminated.

Beating the sword when it was red hot tested the integrity of it before it was taken into battle. A trained Roman soldier needed the assurance that in battle his sword would not break under the constant pounding because his life depended on it.

Champions of life have submitted themselves to the creative process of perfection. They are not interested in going into life's battle without first being battle tested. These champions in life have endured the constant pounding of a disciplined, regimented training and have been qualified and declared duly ready to overcome the challenges in their lives. In an actual battle, it is too late to test what should have been tested and examined in training. Honesty and durability describe what integrity is, but maintaining and overcoming illustrates what integrity does.

Power words for Integrity: Honesty, completeness, purity, stability, incorruption, straightforwardness, soundness, absoluteness, and forthrightness.

O is for Optimism

Optimism without faith is like a frame without a picture.

We live in a society where most people are symmetrically opposed to positive people. A person who is optimistic about a negative situation often aggravates those individuals who are pessimistic in nature. Negative people can give you a hundred reasons why you cannot succeed in your endeavors. They will start off with all the obvious external blemishes and then they will attack your character and heart. Skeptics always believe that they have more going for themselves than you have working for you. And despite your achievements, they will never allow themselves to see you any higher than they at their lowest point. This is one good reason why you should not waste your time trying to make a liar out of your critics. Instead, make a believer out of yourself. If there is anybody who needs to be convinced about your ability to succeed—it is you! If you are convinced about your abilities and you believe in you, why should you care about what others think? Your greatest victory will not come in your challenge with other people; it will only happen after you've conquered your own fears and insecurities.

Optimism is expectancy in its most generic form. OPTIMISM is an active, empowering, constructive attitude that creates conditions for success by focusing and acting on possibilities and opportunities. If a person desires to live effectively, he or she will have to root out all self-defeating pessimism and replace it with active enthusiasm.

True optimism is not forcing a smile in order to convince others that all is well. This will simply be a surface mask intended to camouflage your confusion and frustration. Once you fully understand and are persuaded of why negativity holds you back, you will be able to live practical and productive lives for the better.

Christians, pastors, businessmen, athletes, dancers, recording artists, actors and actresses, etc. are all vulnerable to the attacks of pessimism. Your greatest vulnerability to the attacks of jealousy and negativity will always stem from the success of someone in your own field of expertise. A person is seldom envious of someone in another field.

Christians should be the most positive people on the planet. Over time, some of us have only proven to be among the most negative in society. But in all actuality Christians have an active living faith residing inside of them that reveals the truth that nothing is impossible to them that believe. What a living legacy.

Champions of life are people who rise to the occasion when a negative situation arises. They have forecasted the outcome because they've calculated the win. It is important to realize life is like a battery—it needs both positive and negative connections in order to tap into its benefits and rewards.

Power words for Optimism: Anticipation, possible, happiness, idealism, positivism, resilience, cheerfulness, and enthusiasm.

N is for Notable

People of notable character are those who have done the insignificant, overlooked things for people less fortunate than themselves, which distinguishes them from the rich and famous.

Mother Teresa spent her entire life touching the lives of people who could not in turn reward her with anything but a smile and a thank you. Martin Luther King, Jr. lost his life fighting for equality for all African Americans and under privileged people in America, in spite of their race, creed, or color. Jesus did not spend the bulk of His time in ministry raising funds to support His missionary efforts. His ministry was supported and funded by those who were delivered of demons, healed of sicknesses and diseases and forgiven of their sins. He reached out to touch the forgotten and told them that God knew them by name; He preached the good news to the poor and exposed them to how to prosper; Jesus also motivated change in women that laid on their backs for a living and showed them a better way to make a living and feel good about themselves. And at the end of His human life on earth and in taking His last breath, He exclaimed, "Forgive them for they know not what they do."

Which act deserves the most distinguished reward, the work of Jesus Christ or the singing career and antics of Elvis Presley? In truth, no other act should be mentioned in the same breath with Jesus. People are noteworthy for the noble things they have done in the lives of people, not for the things they have done in order to boost their careers.

Our society is so shallow that it reveals its ugly head in most people who are only interested in becoming rich and famous. Television presents the wrong message to our kids, leaving them with few options but many inconsistencies. Moreover, adults are inundated with images of extra-marital affairs, killings, anger management problems, integrity issues in our White House, and white collar crimes where only 1 out of every 100 persons found guilty spends time in prison.

People do not generally desire to live a life of principle. They want money and fame even at the cost of their honor. Being rich and/or famous does not improve your character, nor does it eliminate your shortcomings. In these

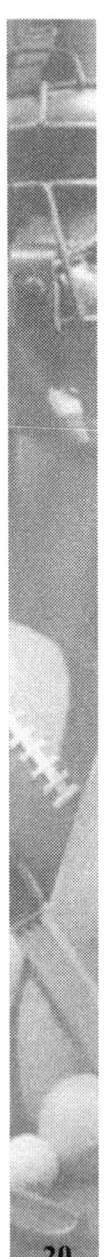

modern times, some people can become famous by acting a complete fool.

Champions of life are not shallow people looking for someone to acknowledge their noble deeds. In fact, they do not post them on the front page of the newspaper trying to get the attention of the public. A person may only hear what a Champion is doing in the lives of others, from those who are direct or indirect recipients of their labor of love. Champions stand for a cause, they are not rebels without a cause.

Find a hurting person and meet their need. You don't have to look far to find a lonely person. Mark the life of the lonely with your companionship. Become interested in other people's lives and watch how they will celebrate your presence.

Power words for Notable: Worthy, remarkable, prominent, distinguished, noteworthy, memorable, nameable, renowned, and illustrious.

Chapter 2

Changing Men in Changing Times

Chapter 2

Changing Men In Changing Times

The word *creative* has become an old favorite among people who like to think of themselves as such. People use this word in their vocabulary whether they can define it or not. Creativity is expected of ministers, advertising copywriters, people in the entertainment industry, fashion designers and the list can go on and on. In this fast pace, money driven society that we live in, if you're not certified "creative," your opportunities are slim and your future is in big trouble.

The truth of the matter is that no one is truly creative. We live in a closed universe and the Bible is quite clear on the fact that there is nothing new under the sun. Instead of being creative, we are instead *inventive*. We simply rearrange and reposition things that have already been created.

Although I will use the words *creative* and *creativity,* please keep in mind that what I am actually referencing is the word ingenuity or inventiveness. God alone has the ability to create and humans can only reposition or rearrange what is already done. This is creativity, but not in the essence of creating.

Creativity has to do with more than just architecture, art, music, or writing. Creativity can be exemplified through survival tactics. When a man loses his transitional quality in a changing market, a changing culture, and a changing world, not only will he not keep up with the times for which he lives, he will not survive it.

We are living in times where there is an acceleration of change. Nothing seems to remain the same more than a year at a time. What are causing such changes are not men, but rather their inventions.

1. Automobiles have become faster.
2. Planes are faster and more sophisticated.
3. Computers started with kilobytes, then Megabytes, Gigabytes, and now Terabytes.
4. Cooking on the stove is nearly obsolete because of microwaves and convection ovens.

5. Money is changing hands quicker than you can get it.

Nothing is moving at a normal pace and if you do, you will get run over or left behind. The most important thing in life is not to concentrate on trying to keep up because of the dollars being jeopardized, but because you want to be a man living in the time frame for which you presently exist. The important thing is to profit mentally, emotionally, spiritually, and physically from these new times. Today's youth understand electronics, computers, and internet, but most men over 50 do not speak the technological language of today. Being relevant is the key to a man's expression of growth. Leaders get out in front and stay there by raising the standards by which they judge themselves and by which they are willing to be judged.

There are many men who are silent sufferers. They suffer with low self-esteem, insecurities, jealousy, anger, fears, childhood nightmares, and so much more. And until many of us stop hiding like Adam, we will never discover our true worth as men. After the personality has faded, the only thing that will be exposed is your character or the lack of it. You can't get respect, hiding like a coward.

> Responsibilities don't dissipate, they only change hands.

God commits to men of character, not talent. The Bible speaks of fathers, the world speaks of mentors. What's the difference? Mentors assume the responsibility of a teacher with shallow qualifications. Fathers assume the responsibility to parent with heaven qualities that are non-negotiable. A basic tenet of fathering is teaching sons and daughters to accept responsibility for their actions. They realize that children normally do what they see being done, not by the instructions given to them. The father becomes the standard for success in life, family, and business. A lie today is still a lie tomorrow. Responsibilities don't dissipate, they only change hands. True of Adam to Eve and Eve to Satan! We appropriately call this "passing the buck."

Society is constantly changing! But the only thing that should not change in a man's life is the godly principles by which he chooses to conduct his life. Some fifteen years ago, I had this eye opening experience while praying. I used to cheat while playing monopoly. I didn't think anything of it because it was just a game. Of course, I did not feel completely good about myself when I won a game after

cheating, but I would quickly get over it. Since I was usually selected to be the banker, I would steal the needed funds in order to buy more property or pay any debts for landing on someone else's property. One day as I was praying, I distinctly heard a voice say to me, "If you cheat in monopoly, you will cheat in life." I didn't question the voice because I knew that it was the Lord, and besides, the devil would never inform or correct something that is right and godly. I realized then that changing bad habits is the key to having a fresh new beginning. I stopped cheating and my life has never been the same.

When I was a young Buck Sergeant in the U.S. Army, I had another experience that revolutionized my life. My boss, who was the meanest Master Sergeant I thought that I had ever met in my life, was transferring to a new Army Unit. Just when I became successful in learning his system and how to lead my section the way he wanted it, he received orders to leave. When his replacement came in, I was certain that this new Master Sergeant was meaner and more inconsiderate than the former one. He made many changes in our Communications section that caused a tremendous ruckus. Nevertheless, we had to adapt and function accordingly. It was my job to acclimate my men to this new system which proved to push all of us to excel. No one likes change, but change is inevitable.

I recall going on a field exercise (play army) and was asked to have my men produce directional antennas for a Howitzer Unit. I didn't have a clue as to how to perform such a task. You see, the Army doesn't have time to train a soldier on everything that he or she should know concerning their specific job, so they provide Training Manuals (TM). My men were as baffled as I was when the Master Sergeant initially gave me an order to perform such a task. I must have looked like I was trying to interpret Greek, which I don't speak. So I gathered enough nerve to tell my Sergeant a thing or two. I went to him and said, "I was never trained on such a device and I don't have a clue as to how to begin." He looked at me and said with a sarcastic voice, "Look in your Training Manual, Sergeant." Well, first of all, we never took training manuals to the field and secondly we didn't have any training manuals provided. But this Master Sergeant was prepared because he was accustomed to helping soldiers to become better at what they do. He provided me with all the necessary training manuals and tools in order to properly do my job and train my men. From

> When a man is willing to change, he is willing to grow.

that point on, I never questioned another motive of his. He raised the bar and I reached for it and began to develop myself on a more professional level. When a man is willing to change, he is willing to grow. Never tell a person to do something without giving him the tools to perform it.

Chapter 3

The Portrait of a Leader

Chapter 3

The Portrait of a Leader

Every person is a leader of some sort, but what kind of leader they are depends on the qualities that exude from their personality. From the vagabond on the streets to the president in the White House, every person is a leader. The title before a man's name means absolutely nothing, nor does a person's background. Men don't honor titles, they honor deeds.

> Men don't honor titles, they honor deeds.

Dr. Martin Luther King, Jr. labored intensively traveling across the United States fighting racial prejudices and injustice toward African Americans. He was not just a great orator, but a great leader of the people. He rallied men of all races and religious backgrounds together for a common cause which has not been duplicated to this day. Winston Churchill was not only a charismatic leader and spokesman for Great Britain, but he displayed the posture of a great leader and the qualities of a winner. He allied with the Americans during WWII then challenged other European nations to do the same. Former president Franklin D. Roosevelt had such a profound respect for Winston Churchill that even he voiced his sentiments on how they could talk for hours and how he enjoyed every minute of it.

If you were to ask 100 men about their leadership qualities and how they feel they would fare if judged by their contemporaries, 97 out of 100 would probably give themselves a passing grade. Usually men don't have any problems seeing themselves as leaders; the problem is in leaders seeing themselves as men. What a man says he is, is more often than not, different from what he is. When man sentences himself as a failure, he is judging himself by his actions. What you become as a result of your actions in life does not mean that your actions truly dictate who you are. Your actions simply indicate your present state of mind.

Every man has at one time or another experienced a thought of being a captain of men. As young boys playing GI Joe, we would lead the other toy soldiers into battle and capture the land and set the captives free. Yet, as we grew into adolescence we slowly discovered the challenges of a leader. If you played any kind of sports as a lad, you saw the pressures and the glory of the team's star player. With leadership come pressures and choices, glory and accolades, and sweat and tears. I often hear young men say to me, "I would never want your job!" My response to many of them would be, "Then you don't want to be a leader." It's not the job these young men are trying to evade, it is the pressures, the headaches and responsibilities they are not interested in having.

What separates leaders? Good question. Is it the titles such as, CEO, President, COO, Chief, Coach, Pastor, or Quarterback? Titles do not define your leadership qualities; titles describe the perimeters or range of their authority. Leaders are classified in three categories; *Bad Leader*, *Good Leader*, and *Great Leader*.

> Titles do not define your leadership qualities; titles describe the perimeters or range of their authority.

A bad leader can do good things, just like a good or great leader can do a bad thing, but one or two inconsequential errors do not define your entire career as a leader. Being a great leader is not solely based on how many battles have been won or how many men are being led into battle. In this present day society, people secretly judge others' leadership skills by numbers. This would be quite silly, because an evil leader can lead millions and can subdue nations, but he himself can be completely incompetent in winning internal battles over jealousy, illicit sexual appetite and hatred. Adolf Hitler was such a leader. He was a great strategist and a brilliant military mind and motivator, but he was a very insecure man. Men who walk in insecurity will inevitably try to destroy those who he feels threatened by. The end result to Adolf Hitler's kind of leadership lead to his own generals trying to kill him. One Bible character, King Saul, wanted to be great at the expense of his people. King David, Saul's nemesis, wanted the nation to be great at his own expense.

You don't have to lead an Army Regiment of 50,000 men in order to be classified as a good leader. Good leaders are good followers and bad leaders are bad followers. Every person has the potential to become great leaders, but what holds many back from achieving such an honor is their unwillingness to be a person of convictions. Convictions are non-negotiable while a person's preference can be easily up for bids. Both good and great leaders are those whose convictions are the standards by which they govern their lives. Great leaders do not set out to become great leaders; they just want to do a great job.

What qualifies and separates these various kinds of leaders? How can men play a crucial part in developing other men into good leaders? If a person is already in a leadership role and has not discovered his identity, this leader will destroy many men and women with their authority. I will put down different attributes of all three kinds of leaders and hope that in the process of reading this you will identify what kind of leader you are and how you can better yourself as a leader.

Good Leader	Bad Leader	Great Leader
1. Confidence	Arrogance	Faith
2. Submission	Resistence	Relinquish
3. Boldness	Reluctance	Audacity
4. Bravery	Cowardice	Courage
5. Seeks knowledge	Rejects knowledge	Loves knowledge
6. Enthusiasm	Negativity	Positive
7. Self-respect	Self-doubt	Healthy God esteem
8. Fights for Cause	Rebel without a Cause	Stands for Cause
9. Fidelity to God	Fidelity to Self	Fidelity to God & Men

A bad leader does not have to remain a bad leader. They can easily become good leaders if they would divorce themselves from any and all of these horrible attributes that characterize a bad leader. Good qualities are important in order to become a great leader. Each person must work hard to establish these good qualities because human nature is basically evil and self-centered. As you learn of what truly matters to you, it can become a gauge to help you discover where you are in the leadership development process.

Men have asked me about my leadership qualities and how I developed them. One man who was apparently very jealous of me became very angry when he saw the respect that the men had for me and how they responded to me with "Yes Sir, No Sir." He asked me, "Why do you have these people bowing down to you and calling you sir?" My reply was simple. "I never asked them to call me sir, nor did I ever verbally demand respect from them." Real men recognize good leaders even if they themselves are poor leaders. A great leader has an ambience of confidence and certainty. They don't try to be great leaders, they just are.

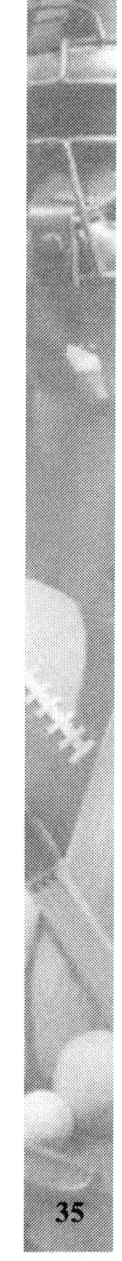

Developing A Champion Spirit – in just 10 minutes

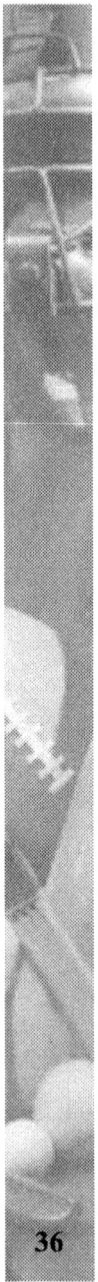

Chapter 4

Exercising Your Power to Dominate

Chapter 4

Exercising Your Power to Dominate

When I think of all the tools that God has placed within our hands as men to fulfill our purpose in life, I can't help but see how we squander those very tools and surrender our choices foolishly. God has gone through great lengths to meticulously create us. Within our bodies are cells to fight off alien cells that are invading our body. In the same way, there are basic things we can do to ensure our success in spite of the opposition.

There was a study done by the Department of Health, Education, and Welfare that stated that out of every 100 people starting their career the following situations exist at age 65.

- **29 are dead**
- **13 have annual incomes of $3,500 to $4,500 (which is below the poverty level)**
- **55 have annual incomes from $4,500**

to $20,000 (the median income is $5,700)
- 3 have annual incomes over $29,000.

They estimate that 2 out of 10 families have specific goals to chart where their family will end up. The other families are playing Russian roulette with their lives. Failing to plan and chart your course for life is planning to fail.

Here are three things that are sure to cause you to miss the mark for your life and leave you as an unguarded target for destruction.

1. LAZINESS—apathy, idleness, inactivity, lethargy

> **Pr 24:30** I went past the field of the sluggard, past the vineyard of the man who lacks judgment;
> **Pr 24:31** thorns had come up everywhere, the ground was covered with weeds, and the stone wall was in ruins.
> **Pr 24:32** I applied my heart to what I observed and learned a lesson from what I saw:
> **Pr 24:33** A little sleep, a little slumber, a little folding of the hands to rest--
> **Pr 24:34** and poverty will come on you like a bandit and scarcity like an

armed man. (NIV)

2. PROCRASTINATION—delay, postpone, put off, drag your feet

Eccles 5:4 When you make a vow to God, do not delay in fulfilling it. He has no pleasure in fools; fulfill your vow. (NIV)

Mt 8:21 Another disciple said to him, "Lord, first let me go and bury my father." (NIV)
Mt 8:22 But Jesus told him, "Follow me, and let the dead bury their own dead." (NIV)

Both procrastinators and lazy people are usually playing catch up, but they never do. They allow their problems to get so far ahead that a solution cannot draw near. I have learned that in leading and being a leader, you cannot weigh and assess every problem before making a decision. There are times when time is of the essence. Procrastinators claim that the reason why they are procrastinating is so that they can make the best decision possible. Making no decision is still a decision. The promise land

> Making no decision is still a decision.

> **Don't assess, when it's time to possess!**

for the Israelites was delayed forty years because ten of the spies assessed the land as hostile and filled with giants. Don't assess, when it's time to possess!

3. LACK OF KNOWLEDGE

> **Ho 4:6** my people are destroyed from lack of knowledge. "Because you have rejected knowledge, I also reject you as my priests; because you have ignored the law of your God, I also will ignore your children. (NIV)

These are people that are always learning and asking more questions, but they never come into the knowledge of the truth. It's not that these people are brainless; they feel that the information is insignificant. Sometimes, asking question after question is only a diversionary tactic to avoid the challenge.

Every child goes through the basic course of learning perseverance. It is a part of your natural prohibition against **uncertainty**. How you develop it growing into your adult years is your responsibility. An infant learns that if they cry enough they will get the attention of the parent. Between three to five months the child begins to reach for things. If you take something from a child, the child reaches out for it despite your trying to keep it from them. To stop them from reaching for the item, the person would have to hide it from them. It is in every man to persevere.

Men are natural sports fanatics. Case and point, my son was three years old when he started watching sports with me. My wife and I would notice that by the time he was five, I could leave him in the living room to get some refreshments, return ten minutes later and he would be deeply engrossed into the game. I thought maybe this could not be possible because he was too young to understand the game. I discovered that it wasn't the rules of the game; it was the competition of the game that attracted him. Today, he is very competitive in every kind of sport and video game he plays. Aggression usually dominates a man's nature. There is nothing wrong with wanting to win; it is simply how you play the game that matters. Life is not a game, but there are rules to it, and if you are going to experience any success in life, you must abide by the rules that governs success.

Dominion is the next step in life. Children are natural dominators. God gave us this ability before we were ever born because He told us to dominate and subdue the earth. Before God created the body of mankind, He spoke into the man's DNA and placed the ability to dominate there. When Adam sinned in the garden and passed over his dominion to Eve and Eve passed it to Satan, they were giving Satan the right to dominate mankind.

> There is nothing wrong with wanting to win; it is simply how you play the game that matters.

POINT: God has not taken dominion away, He simply took man's access to Him away because of sin. Man lost relationship and understanding which was necessary to exercise dominion properly. From there, the condition deteriorated as a man, now he voluntarily gives himself over to the dominion of others. The original Man (Adam) actually violated the law of responsibility.

From 1981 to the present in the United States, the cost of tobacco almost doubled from 25 billion to 45 billion; Alcohol from 37 billion to 62 billion; Marijuana 24 billion to 50 billion; Cocaine 35 billion to 75 billion. And well over half of America's staggering 300 billion dollar medical cost can be attributed to illnesses induced by slavery to these items. These figures are only illustrative of the financial toll we pay each year for our loss of dominion. When man is not under God's authority he has

no control of himself. If man is going to exercise dominion, he must first be free to do so.

When men working through a relationship with Jesus learn to reestablish God's dominion over himself, then, he is capable of reestablishing his God-given dominion over everything else.

> **Prov 16:32** He that is slow to anger is better than the mighty; and he that ruleth his spirit than he that taketh a city. (KJV)

> **Prov 25:28** He that hath no rule over his own spirit is like a city that is broken down, and without walls. (KJV)

In order to overcome our own passions, it requires more steady management than obtaining victory over an opponent. The man that has rule over his own spirit maintains the government of himself, and of his own appetites and passions, and does not suffer them to rebel against reason and conscience. He has the rule of his own thoughts, his desires, his inclinations, his resentments, and keeps them all in good order. The bad case of a vicious man, who has not this rule over his own spirit, who, when temptations to excess in eating or drinking are before him, has no government of himself; when he is provoked he breaks out into exorbitant passions, such a one is like a city that is broken down and without walls. All that is good goes out and forsakes him; all that is evil breaks in upon him. He lies exposed to all the temptations of life and becomes an easy prey for his enemies.

Have you ever known people that the slightest thing sets them off? They let their thoughts dictate to their emotions.

> **Prov 18:19** An offended (upset, displeased) brother is more unyielding than a fortified city, and disputes are like the barred gates of a citadel. (NIV)

When a person becomes offended by truth or lies and shut themselves off because of a stubborn will, then there is a root of bitterness so deeply embedded that nothing can pull them out of their stance. Not even God can pull them out of their stubbornness. God will not force a person to do what is right! They are the only ones who can pull themselves out because they must forgive in order to be free from their anger.

Men love to overcome obstacles, but they

often have a difficult time overpowering their passions. Life is not a sport nor is it a game. And life is certainly not a rehearsal. Therefore, in order to win in life, we must be willing to be mentored, trained or coached by the most respected person in our rolodex. With all the raw talent and power of a man, he needs to learn how to harness his power and pick his battles well. This, my friend, doesn't come with age. I have known some old fools in my day as well as young ones.

I am a diehard Los Angeles Lakers fan and nothing baffled me in sports like that of the trade of Shaquille O'Neal of the 2004 season. Kobe Bryant was just coming out of his legal battles and seemingly entering into a new battle with a Los Angeles Lakers teammate and coach. I might be ridiculed for this statement by all those sipping on "hater-rade," but Kobe Bryant is certainly a driving force on the basketball court, but a terrible enforcer in life. Please don't misunderstand me, I do not believe in throwing the baby out along with the dirty bath water. We have all done things that we are ashamed of, and the only difference between Kobe and other men is that most of us have not been caught.

Kobe Bryant is a young man that may not have had anyone in his life that he truly respected and that had the ability to put him in his place.

Of course, he had his father, but not many young men truly respect their father in many areas of life because like most men, we compare; and a father's comparison is not exempt. Coaching a player on the basketball court is not the same as mentoring a man throughout his life. The principles of life can cross over onto the basketball court, but the principles of playing the game of basketball does not exactly cross over into the life factor.

If I had 50 minutes with Kobe Bryant, I would not ask him to tell me about his basketball game and what he thought of the Lakers possibility of going to the playoffs. I would not ask him to tell me about his feelings towards Shaquille O'Neal or Phil Jackson. I would simply ask him to talk truthfully about himself and what's in his heart. Kobe is a man like every other man, he just has more money than most. I am certain that he has already discovered that money is not the key ingredient of life. If a man does not have the respect as a man, it can make him feel lower than most.

Kobe is my-main man. My wife and I love him as a person despite his basketball prowess. Kobe Bryant needs a life-coach or a father-mentor who he respects. A mentor doesn't come to a man and forcibly become a man's mentor or father. An individual must carefully select a person who they have qualified to speak into their life. I don't believe that a person should be selected based on popularity or notoriety. A person might be good for one person, but have nothing to offer another man. We men make many mistakes by choosing someone as a mentor that may already be a guru to the "stars"—thinking that the person might be good for us. I chose a man as a mentor after meeting him one time and I spent three days, no more than 3 to 4 hours a day, pouring out my heart. I knew that this man was not interested in money because he showed a genuine concern for me as a person. He is not well known in popular circles, but highly respected when met for the first time. There is a wisdom that exudes from his being that I captured the first time we met and my life has never been the same. I cannot begin to count how many tears I cried in his presence. But rest assured, I have never felt threatened by him or as though I owed him anything. This is a true mentor and father who helped me regain my dominion and recapture my dreams. Self-respect and self-love is far greater than all the hate in the world.

> Self-respect and self-love is far greater than all the hate in the world.

Men, arise and shine for the glory of the LORD

has risen upon you! No man is an island that includes even YOU!

Developing A Champion Spirit – in just 10 minutes

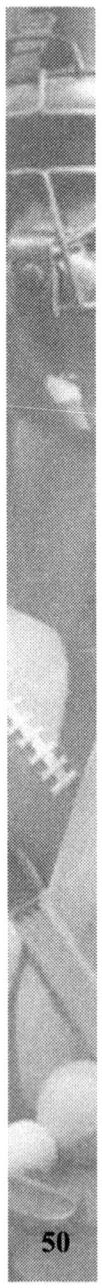

Chapter 5

Principles for Commanding Mountains & Overcoming Obstacles

Chapter 5

Principles for Commanding Mountains & Overcoming Obstacles

The strength of a man is discovered in the principles that govern his life. It is not how well you live it, but by what principles do you live. The most practical success-building wisdom is found in that biblical quotation stating that faith can move mountains. If you really believe that you can move a mountain, then you can. Not many people believe that they can move mountains. Consequently, not many people do. The ones who feel like they cannot move mountains are those who listen to the rationale of the mind which dictates the impossibilities.

> *The strength of a man is discovered in the principles that govern his life.*

Mark 9:23 ..."Everything is possible for him who believes." **(NIV)**

Mark 10:27 Jesus looked at them and said, "With man this is impossible, but not with God; all things are possible with God." (NIV)

These Bible verses dictate the perimeter of possibilities. Knowledge is the acquisition of facts. Understanding is the interpreting of facts which helps in acclimating to these truths; wisdom is the application of facts that helps in determining why, when, and how these truths can be applied. Fact is simply acquiring data or information so that belief and decisions can be made based on substantiated truth. You will never move beyond your accumulation of information. The data that you receive today will determine your location for tomorrow.

> The data that you receive today will determine your location for tomorrow.

Your belief system is not only based on what you have seen, but also on what you have heard and perceived to be truth. Some people believe that Santa Claus is real. If you have come to believe the lie told to you since your childhood, then as far as you are concerned, that lie is truth. You will only do what you believe you can do and all the other challenges will simply conquer you because you don't believe that you are capable of overcoming them.

> **Mark 11:22** "Have faith in God," Jesus answered.
> **23** "I tell you the truth, if anyone says to this mountain, `Go, throw yourself into the sea,' and does not doubt in his heart but believes that what he says will happen, it will be done for him. (NIV)

If you only have faith in God...this is the absolute truth...you can say to this Mount of Olives, `Rise up and fall into the Mediterranean,' and your command will be obeyed. All that is required is that you really believe and have no doubt! You can pray for anything, and if you believe, you have it; it's yours! You must believe that they are yours from the time you ask for them. They simultaneously exist in both the spoken (spiritual) and reality (natural). The person that is successful in life believes that he is a success.

> **Expectancy is the atmosphere which is conducive for change.**

> "The person who thinks he can and the person that thinks he can't are both right."   *--Henry Ford*

The test of your faith is your ability to believe and see the finished product before it is consummated. We are motivated to become what we believe or imagine ourselves to be. Expectancy is the atmosphere which is conducive for change. Mike Murdock said, "You can dig your grave with your mouth or you can build your palace with it." You will speak what you believe, for out of the abundance of the heart the mouth speaks what is believed in the heart.

> Life management begins when you understand the importance of time management.

Life management begins when you understand the importance of time management. Time is the essential ingredient to an individual experiencing success. Life is composed of our choices and constructed by our words. Sometimes, it takes repetition and more repetition for something to develop into a system. Systems are not developed when something is done once, but over and over. Success is in your hands. Do not allow others to create your world with their words, for when they do, they will always make it too small for you.

> Success is in your hands.

Developing A Champion Spirit – in just 10 minutes

All men experience challenges. It's how you handle those challenges that separate the men from the boys. Some challenges present an image that seems to be too powerful to overcome, but this is not a reason to throw in the towel. Fear is not an option! When one fears, he actually believes his fear will materialize. What you submit to grows stronger but what you resist diminishes in strength.

Most men either ignore or are unfamiliar with the process of reciprocity or the law of result. The reason why I know this is because many of them question the size of their return. In order to get a little you must have first given a little. If you want to receive much, you determine it by giving much. The same principle applies to life; junk in, junk out. If a basketball player wants to develop into a great player, he must comply with the law of development. This means that he must not settle at the level of being good. All NBA players are considered good, but only a few are great. Good is often the enemy of best. If you settle at the level of being good, you will never achieve your best. You can have more in life if you simply refuse to settle

> If you settle at the level of being good, you will never achieve your best.

for less. Agreeing with these principles is the first step towards a greater you! Agreement produces power; disagreement results in impotence.

What you believe about God has the greatest potential for good or harm in your life. Everything God does is according to a pattern and based on a principle of His kingdom. The true test of what you believe is not in what you do publicly, but in what you think when you're all alone.

When I speak to my mountains and command them to throw themselves in the sea, what I am saying is "Mountain, get out of my life!" and the mountain must move. God did not give me the grace to climb the mountain; He gave me the grace to command it!

The people who supported you in your endeavors can be tremendous pillars to your success. But those pillars which once supported you can also become obstacles. Oftentimes, people become blindsided when the blockages in life turn out to be the people they love. In order to be a true champion in life, sometimes it means overcoming people. Yes, even those who once helped you, but now feel as though you owe them the world.

A father once said to his son, "Son, I

did a lot for you. I sacrificed my career and forfeited my opportunity to go away to college because I wanted my children to have a father and besides I loved your mother very much. You owe me to do the same with your life and go to college to become a doctor."

Some years later after the son graduated from medical school and had a successful medical practice; he went home to visit his parents.

Son, "Mom, Dad, I'm not going to continue my practice in the medical profession. I decided to quit."

"Why?" said the father. "Haven't we been through this before? We didn't sacrifice for you to do anything but become a doctor."

The son replied, "Dad, what you did was what you wanted to do. I was your son and you brought me into this world. You owe me! You were required to do what you did. You never asked me once what I wanted to do. For once in my life, I am going to do what I truly love doing, and that is my music."

> You can be a success at what others want you to do, but you can never be happy until you do what you have a love to do.

The story ends with the son investing his money in studio equipment and he produced records for artist that sold millions on the pop chart. You can be a success at what others want you to do, but you can never be happy until you do what you have a love to do.

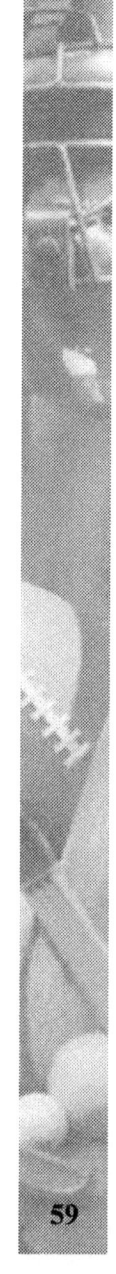

Developing A Champion Spirit – in just 10 minutes

Medallions of Honor

Chapter 2 "Changing Men in Changing Times"
◆ Responsibilities don't dissipate, they only change hands.

◆ When a man is willing to change, he is willing to grow.

Chapter 3 "The Portrait of a Leader"
◆ Men don't honor titles, they honor deeds.

◆ Titles do not define your leadership qualities; titles describe the perimeters or range of their authority.

Chapter 4 "Exercising Your Power to Dominate"
◆ Making no decision is still a decision made. Don't assess, when it's time to possess!

◆ There is nothing wrong with wanting to win; it is simply how you play the game that matters.

◆ Self-respect and self-love is far greater than all the hate in the world.

Chapter 5 "Principles for Commanding Mountains and Overcoming Obstacles"
◆ The strength of a man is discovered in the

principles that govern his life.

◆ The data that you receive today will determine your location for tomorrow.

◆ Expectancy is the atmosphere which is conducive for change.

◆ Life management begins when you understand the importance of time management.

◆ Success is in your hands.

◆ If you settle at the level of being good, you will never achieve your best.

◆ You can be a success at what others want you to do, but you can never be happy until you do what you have a love to do.

Notes

Notes

About the Author

Dr. Mikel Brown is an author, businessman, and religious leader who resides in El Paso, Texas with his wife and two children. He is the President and CEO of CJC Enterprises and owner and CEO of Power Communications Network, through which he conduct seminars and special events. His much sought after style of communicating and humor has made him a favorite for business conclaves and church conventions.

The 3 Secrets of Money

You can hear "The 3 Secrets of Money" absolutely FREE. All you have to do is log on to www.buildinguwealth.com and scroll to the bottom right and click.

Testimonials

I listened to the online lecture at least three times just to gain a proper and healthy perspective of money. I'm making more money than ever before with my talents.

--Musician

Attracting more money has never been easier! The knowledge gained from this lecture caused me to take a introspection of why my income wasn't increasing. Having the knowledge about money is money in the bank.

--Teacher/Business Owner

Visit my website at www.BuildingUWealth.com or www.DreamMakers99.com and discover how you can start living your business dreams of tomorrow, today! Gain the competitive edge by becoming a Dream Makers 99 Associate today!

Log on to www.BuildingUWealth.com and start your dream business.

NEW RELEASES

3 Powerful New Books from Dr. Mikel Brown

Gods Wants You Healthy, Wealthy, & Full of Life

Your capacity to achieve, to have the life you want to have, to be the person you want to be will increase tenfold, because after reading this book you will then possess the keys to a better life. Knowing these special tips will make you more powerful and your life will change for the better.

$11.99

Developing a Champion Spirit - in just 10 Minutes for Women Only

The Greatest Gold-Mine Of Easy Advice For Women Ever Crammed Into One Book!!

Check out the table of Contents:
- Developing the Champion in You
- Women Overcoming Self-Doubt
- His Money is Your Business
- Understanding the Principle of Money
- The New Power Women
- Secrets to Personal Success

$9.95

Developing a Champion Spirit - in just 10 Minutes for Men Only

How to Accomplish Anything You Want in Life.

Check out the table of Contents:
- Developing the Champion in You
- Changing Men in Changing Times
- The Portrait of a Leader
- Exercising Your Power to Dominate
- Principles for Commanding Mountains and Overcoming Obstacles

$9.95

Beyond Ordinary -- Success is Only A Thought Away

The Average Person's Textbook, The Rich Man's Manual.

Your treasure is safe and secured, neatly stored away in your mind. You have a treasure that is presently producing nominal success; "Beyond Ordinary" will show you how to manufacture materially what is in you mentally and spiritually.

If Bill Gates, Michael Jordan, Oprah Winfrey, Donald Trump, Dr. Mikel Brown, or TD Jakes can do it; you can do it, too!

$11.99

..Money Matters..

This Powerful Package will unleash the Financial Harvest in your lifetime!

- ▶ Start Building Your Personal WealthFoundation

- ▶ Gain Confidence To Start Living Your Dreams

- ▶ Building Wealth Success Budget Worksheets

- ▶ Learn The Ten Commandments of Money

- ▶ Break The Mentality of "Just Enough'

Only $55.00

www.BuildingUWealth.com

Power Comminacaitions Newtork * 1208 Sumac Dr* El Paso, Tx 79925

www.ingramcontent.com/pod-product-compliance
Lightning Source LLC
Chambersburg PA
CBHW060341080526
44584CB00013B/868